I'M THAT KID

-

Empowering You to Step into Your Power™ Part 2

TRAY-SEAN BEN SALMI

AKA

CHILD GENIUS ADVISOR

AMAZON #1 BEST SELLER, AWARD
WINNING AUTHOR
AS SEEN ON RADIO & TELEVISION

Published by Influencer Publishing in 2019

Second Edition

'YOU' called this book to you because you live in an ever-changing world and you want to be a part of that change. Everything starts with an idea or concept in your mind. The idea or concept is given form by taking action and manifesting your **dream**s. Then the magic begins to happen during the construction process. That process begins here and **now**!

This book is dedicated to children and youth everywhere...

This book is not intended to provide personalised legal, financial or investment advice. The Author and the Publisher specifically disclaim any liability, loss or rick which is incurred therefore, directly or indirectly, of the use and application of any content of this work.

Cover Design by Swiss Graphics

ACKNOWLEDGEMENTS

I would like to thank God for all of my wealth, health, happiness, opportunities, abundance and support that I have received and experienced! I would also like to take this opportunity to thank all the amazing people that have supported me, guided me and taught me along my journey. I really and truly would not be where I am today if it was not for my family and friends.

I would also like to take this opportunity to acknowledge those of you who have delivered adversity to my life because this has made me stronger and inspired me to convert my adversities into empowerment. After all I am who I am today as a direct result of everything I've experienced.

CONTENTS

*Imagine how you'll feel as you finish reading the
last page of this book.*

Foreword

Did you know that Youth unemployment is one of today's biggest global challenges?

Did you know that Youth entrepreneurship offers a solution to the above, because innovative solutions for economic growth among young people is on the increase?

First of all, I would like to identify Tray-Sean Ben Salmi as a 15-year-old teenager that I hold in high regard, not because he's my son but because I truly admire and respect him upon so many levels in the context of business and personal matters. Tray-Sean is a remarkable teenage genius, who boosts a host of wisdom, skills, experience, products, services, unique opportunities and accolades etc. Who I have found to be passionately supportive of the work of others, devoid of triviality, and nobody's fool.

Tray-Sean Ben Salmi, prior to this book, had already made a lasting impact in both academics and his personal development. Would you agree that few teens do in our current climate of media coverage of our teens. He participated in Child Genius and was recognised as 1 out of 20 of the smartest children in the UK for 2017, he then went on to co-author 10 Seconds to Child Genius with Philip Chan and became 1 of 34 selected to sit papers at the prestigious Eton college for Boys. For more information may I suggest that you purchase a copy of his books called 10 Seconds to Child Genius – From Eton Road to Eton College and 10

Seconds to Child Genius – The Road to Child Genius. At the age of 6 years old Tray-Sean launched his first short story competition in school. Tray-Sean was 7 years old when he co-authored Kidz That Dream Big with his older sister Lashai Ben Salmi and the two of them would attend a host of prestigious investment, business development, branding and personal development events. At the time they were the only children in the room. At the age of 11 Tray-Sean was awarded an UnLtd award to run his first event called: I'm That KID – Bridging the Gap Between Fathers & Sons at Arsenal F.C. which provided a unique opportunity for fathers, their sons, Tray-Sean and his step-father and a fundamental resetting of the moral compass. Thanks to Tray-Sean's (and his four siblings) work, in large part, the direction of youth entrepreneurship now is beginning to point away from simply setting up business and towards helping children and young people to activate their sacred gifts, have fun, dream big and make money doing what they love while gaining key life skills, experience and unique opportunities in abundance. As Tray-Sean's mantra says, "I'm That KID – As long as I believe in myself I can be, do and have anything I desire". This, I completely agree to be true because whatever a man thinks of most, that is exactly what he shall create.

This book is exceptional and most clearly deserves to have a very wide readership, I think it should be carefully read by every child aged 5yrs plus both locally and globally. Quite frankly, nobody else could have written this book reason being that the author himself has consistently excelled in academics and having found meaning in his life with a host of mind-blowing achievements to date. What distinguishes this book is the fact that Tray-Sean is incredibly well connected, well informed, and a personal determination shines through every word; Tray-Sean writes with the beauty of poetry. The book is so well written, it actually does deserve the worn cliché that 'I couldn't put the book down'.

Tray-Sean is an old soul in a young body, that is in affect way ahead of his time.

Tray-Sean experienced an extremely traumatic birth, which almost cost him his life. He has faced life threatening respiratory issues since birth which resulted in frequent visits to A&E and has been cared for by several consultants since birth. Tray-Sean was diagnosed with Asthma at the age of 4, the precise context I am referring to the above is to highlight what a 15-year-old can do, not what he or she cannot do despite being seriously ill from birth and had to overcome anxiety and low self-esteem.
I appreciate the sincerity, consistency, commitment, service to others, creativity, courage, passion, compassion, empathy, determination and genuineness of Tray-Sean. This book is written in a 'friendly' style, I especially recommend this book to our friends, family, colleagues and all establishments who work with children and young people. Unfortunately, our teens face a host of challenges as they transition from childhood to adulthood this endeavour should never be at the

expense of the current generation of young people. I believe that the content of this book with inspire children, youth and adults alike to achieve the same or better because Tray-Sean is 'keeping it real' when it comes to highlighting what could be possible when children and youth are allowed to Dream Big as young as possible. We should all be on guard when it comes to protecting our children's natural ability to Dream Big, self-belief and experiential learning.

This book will be invaluable to anyone who wishes to learn about aspects of fully embodying their dream. I know of no other source which matches the quality and breadth of writing as in the book and the other books that Tray-Sean has authored, in a brilliant and unique way; including young onset raw creativity, personal development, self-realisation and experiential learning. And yet the book does not paralyse any approach that you may currently be honouring. I recommend to you his unique chapter on Consequences of Delayed Creativity, for example. Tray's book, overall, takes the field of Youth Entrepreneurship much further forward.

In fact, the book brings up topics that I really wish I was exposed to during my own childhood, because I believe that I could have made much more progress in my life by now. In the areas of developing my core life skills, financial literacy, personal development etc as early as possible. The book further broaches additional topics in a unique, incredible way so as not to make you feel uncomfortable.

One of my favourite parts of the book is About the Author, because this is where Tray-Sean shares what he has achieved to date. I believe that this will inspire others about what is possible when you choose to Dream Big, invest time in personal development and have fun learning.

I feel that through this book Tray-Sean will ultimately reach out to millions, whether they are academic, artistic and/or entrepreneurial. A word I have often heard used about Tray-Sean is 'Inspirational'. In today's society of modern-day materialism in the media, it is not uncommon for this word to be used, but in Tray's case it is richly deserved. Trays acts a focus for acknowledgement for values and attitudes which are right about this world, in generosity and warmth of spirit; of being educated, and great fun to be with. I know that family means a lot to Tray, words cannot possibly convey how proud we are of him for choosing to step into his power and embrace life despite being bullied, having low self-esteem, experiencing panic attacks due to anxiety brought on as a result of health challenges (life threatening asthma attacks). This book is highly original. I think it makes the weather on so many key topics, such as the natural abilities of children being just as capable as adults when it comes to entrepreneurship. Whilst it may make some people feel uncomfortable to embrace youth entrepreneurship, including 'experts' and people in the media. They need not just to hear but to listen carefully to the immense lifelong benefits of youth entrepreneurship and self-exploration. The book somehow combines being timeless, placeless, and yet firmly relevant to us all, in the here and now, and clearly ahead of its time. This inherent child/youth entrepreneurship culture does not particularly worry me, because of the sheer brilliance shared within this book.

I am honoured to be Tray-Sean's mother. He is the second eldest of five siblings and I must say that he inspires me and teaches me so much about life, myself and others upon a daily basis. Inside this book you'll be exposed to a host of inspiring content that could transform your life and that of children and young people around the world.

Therefore, I truly believe that this book is a step in the right direction.

Sabrina Ben Salmi BSc
Co-Founding Director of Harris Invictus, Multiple award-winning Mentor and Author, Speaker, Founder of Shift Happens, Dreaming Big Together - Mamas Secret Recipe™ and co-founder of The Conscious Entrepreneur Blueprint™

INTRODUCTION

I'M THAT KID - EMPOWERING YOU TO STEP INTO YOUR POWER FORMULA™ aims to inspire you to reconnect with your true self and acknowledge your natural strengths and weaknesses.

I felt compelled to write this book because of my own personal journey of self-discovery. When I was growing up at around 6 or 7 years old, I would often overhear adults say that they're on a journey of self-discovery/trying to find themselves. I remember thinking "What is wrong with these adults? How on earth can you lose yourself if you are yourself? You can't lose yourself silly billy". These were all of the thoughts that were running through my mind, because I was too young to fully comprehend what self-discovery was.

Now, that I am 14 years old, I have grown to realise that quite often than not children, teens and adults can become disconnected from themselves, as a result of experiencing significant emotional events which can result in someone feeling as if they've lost themselves because they feel disconnected. I have also grown to believe that the self is not something a person finds, instead it is something one merely becomes aware of once a person chooses to expand their awareness, learn more about their dreams, fears, strengths and weaknesses etc. After all we all experience a host of contrast from time to time. For you it may be problems at school, home, work, a relationship, community, place of worship, financial problems, or just dissatisfaction with your day to day activities or it could even be a combination of all of the above. At times we might not even know exactly what the problem is, and you may simply feel as if something doesn't feel right. Whatever it might be for you, I would like to remind you that every problem has a solution, its merely a matter of perspective and perception. My mum often says that "Life is a journey of market research and what we choose to do with the data is up to us". Ask yourself what you have learned about yourself so far? I truly believe that we can either choose to go through life or we can choose to grow through life. We can either choose to give our attention to things that make us feel good or things that do not, ultimately the choice is ours.

I believe that it is very important to trust yourself and my little brother always says "Stop!, following a compass your whole life because the real compass is inside of you and it's your heart". In life it is very important for you to learn to trust yourself.

I was inspired to write I'm That KID because I went from being extremely shy to appearing on TV, winning awards and talking on stage the moment. That I chose to accept myself because I learned that as long as I believed in myself I could be, do and have anything.

Have you ever said something to someone, even though you knew you should keep your mouth shut? Have you ever known the right thing to do, but done something else because the "right" way was too difficult? Do you have habits that you know you should stop, but can't seem to find the will power to do so? Are you unhappy with your health, even though you know the benefits of exercise and a healthy diet? If you answered yes to any of these questions, don't feel alone.

Growing up can be a confusing process in so many ways because you're often pulled in a multitude of directions, not wanting to disappoint your friends and family.

Each of the chapter titles contained in this book are actual programs that I have created, so please do not hesitate to contact me should you wish to invest in any of my products and services.

I'M THAT KID - BRIDGING THE GAP BETWEEN FATHERS & SONS™

I was awarded an UnLtd award when I was 11years old because of my idea for father and son bonding called I'm That KID – Bridging the Gap Between Fathers & Sons.

The idea came about when I was walking home from school with my mum. I can still remember what I said as if it was yesterday.

Me: Mum, I need a mentor

Mum: Pardon son?

Me: I want to know how to become a man

Mum: Oh, wow son, what do you mean? Talk to me…

Me: Pups is at home, but he doesn't do anything with us, he doesn't show any interest in our lives, he never celebrates us, he always complains and blames others, he has no respect for you and does not support us to build our dreams, he does not appreciate you, he just sits there. His body is at home but his mind and soul is not and it breaks my heart because pups doesn't know how to be a man so how can he teach us? I feel for him because he and many man do not know how to be vulnerable enough to be honest and open about how they are feeling inside so they can address their fears, so they can free themselves from past bondage. Instead they try to pretend that they are not in pain and they choose to live life like a zombie, merely existing.

Mum (emotional): Oh, wow son, I had no idea that you were aware of so much. I love you and I am sorry – I promise that I will do my best to support you and find you a mentor

Me: Thanks mum, I also have an idea – what if I would create a workshop so Pups doesn't feel embarrassed and that way we can learn together

Mum: That's a fantastic idea son

At times its during our darkest moments that our biggest inspiration can be birthed if we surrender to the process. I then applied for an UnLtd award **Denise Ramsey** was my phenomenal project manager) purchased a MacBook with the help of **Majid Khan**, ordered business cards via Vistaprint, setup social media handles, built a free website on Wix, had a logo designed by **Courtney Joseph**, spoke to everyone I knew about my idea, contacted the newspaper, setup a go fund me page to cover the cost of venue hire, asked **Tosin Ogunnusi** for support to develop my USB (Unique Brand System) and on the day for event expertise, setup and board breaking. My family and friends were all there on the day to help me make the event a huge success. It was such an amazing feeling to see the room filling up on the day. **Aidan Lee** and **Ben Green** were two of my volunteers on the day because there were some boys who attended without their fathers and some attended alone. I have so much gratitude for everyone who choose to be in the room and make the day a huge success. There was tears, there were insights, there was breakthroughs and so much more.

If you'd like to view testimonies from the event simply go to YouTube:

Tray-Sean Ben Salmi and then scroll down to videos titled`

Testimony for I'm That Kid – Bridging the Gap Between Fathers & sons

This is what my YouTube channel looks like.

Maxine's Shout
Inspirational message to kids
'Anything is possible' for proactive 10-year-old who designs own T-shirts

BE WITH WHO MAKES
YOU SMILE
LAUGH AS MUCH
AS YOU BREATHE
LOVE AS LONG
AS YOU LIVE

AS YOU BREATHE
LOVE AS LONG
AS YOU LIVE

"I'M THAT KID"

YOUNG CITIZEN

Nurturing the
special bond of
fathers and sons

Affordable Carpet

In the eyes of a son, their father is like their superhero therefore its so important for fathers to be present for their sons. So I suggest that quality time is spent on developing common interests, be playful together as often as possible, participate in local father-son activities, work on a project together, spend quality time together listening to how each of you feel about what is going on in each other's lives so you can develop a strong bond.

At times fathers forget how important it is for their sons to see a father love or at least respects his mother. This shows the son how to treat his mother, his sisters, and all the women he'll meet in his life. What a son observes at home will set the foundation form that which he will grow up to draw from when he's interacting with female-based relationships later in his life.

A son needs to see leadership at home. He needs to see a father leading by example and serving. When a son sees his father leading by serving, he will better understand leadership and be able to more effectively lead instead of following his peers. As he grows up, he will become a better leader in all areas of his life. I truly believe that boys need love and healthy boundaries.

THIS IS MY SPEECH THAT I SHARED FROM STAGE FOR BLACK HISTORY MONTH AT VIRGIN MONEY LOUNGE

*"Hi guys, it has been an amazing day so far and I
have loved the comedy and I would just like to
share with you why black history is important to
me*

*Well black history is important because it allows
me to know I heritage and where I come from
my family lineage and it helps to pave
out my future because of the achievements of my
forefathers who came before me and we use
this **month** to remember
the **important** contributions and
achievements throughout **history***

*Well you might be wondering why I am up here
talking to you and how I can add value to your day.*

*Please relax and take a moment to think about your
relationship with your father. For some of you your
father is your best friend, your hero or even
your role model.*

Unfortunately, things wasn't the same for me…

*Well, I didn't have a good relationship with my
step-dad. You might know what I mean, if I say
that he was there physically but he wasn't present.*

Can you remember a time when you felt invisible?

When you felt left out?

When you felt ignored?

It was very hard for me because I would see people walking past me with their dads laughing and having fun whilst mine was at home ignoring us

It just made it worse for me as I lacked in confidence and was always putting myself down in all aspects and was very hard on myself and not to mention the fact that I was also being bullied in school.

When I was around 10/11 years old, I was walking home with my mum and I asked for a mentor and my mum was flabbergasted. Mum tried her best to find a mentor, but because we couldn't find a mentor my mum took me a long to personal development events where I met Cheryl Chapman who helped me to speak up more and if it wasn't Cheryl I wouldn't be up here speaking to you today

I decided to turn my adversities into empowerment and I created I'm that kid which is about choosing self-acceptance.

As a result of this I started to run events I had my first event at the arsenal hub called "I'M THAT KID - Bridging The Gap Between Fathers & Sons" I did this in a way that wouldn't make me point fingers at my step-dad but as a way so that both of us could learn

All of this confidence has just built up and has allowed me to show my intelligence and I was recently featured in child genius 2017 show (recognised as 1 of 20 smartest children in the UK. I went on to be 1 of 34 boys to invited to sit papers at the prestigious Eton College for Boys) co-author a book with Philip Chan under the brand of 10 Seconds to Child Genius. I'm That KID is growing and I now have services which I desire to use to touch the hearts of many around the world. I'm That KID covers: I'm That KID - Bridging The Gap Between Fathers & Sons™, I'm That KID – Creating A Vision Board for My Future™, I'm That KID – Taking The Stage™, I'm That KID - Inspiring My Community To Pay It Forward™, I'm That KID - There's A Book Inside ME™, I'm That KID - Families That Play Together Stay Together™, I'm That KID - Empowering You To Step Into Your POWER™ and I'm That KID - BEING The Change That I Desires To See In The World™. I have big dreams and I am open to receiving unexpected opportunities in abundance. Thank you so much for listening because together the impossible is possible.

BEN SALMI FAMILY MANTRA

BEN SALMI TEAMWORK, MAKES THE DREAMWORK

We believe that there is no such thing as failure only feedback.

*We also believe that the journey of one thousand
miles begins with a single step in the right
direction*

FAMILY ANTHEM

*If you want to be somebody,
If you want to go somewhere,
You better wake up and PAY ATTENTION*

*I'm ready to be somebody,
I'm ready to go somewhere,
I'm ready to wake up and PAY ATTENTION!*

The question is ARE YOU?

Now I am going to share my Dear Dad Poem,

*I AM your son and I need you now. Please hold my
hand. Stand by my side, tell me that I am good
enough, let me know that you can hear me, that you
are watching the help me get back up each time I
fall. Take time to grow to understand me. Take my
hand daddy and lead me from this place. Please
chase away my doubts, fears and wipe away my
tears. Dear daddy, don't leave me to figure it out all
alone. I need your hand to hold. I need the warmth
of your touch; my world has grown so cold. Please
be a daddy to me and hold me day by day, because
with your loving hand in mine I know we will find a
way."*

Take a moment to reflect upon the relationship that you have with your father and I encourage you to write a letter of expression to either expression gratitude or how you desire for things to improve. Remember only the truth will set you free.

I'M THAT KID - CREATING A VISION BOARD FOR MY FUTURE™

I have several goals and one of my big goals is to become a professional footballer and a neuroscientist.

Over the years each and every mentor that I have had constantly repeated over and over and over again the importance of goal setting. In their own unique way, they'd say that goals are what take us forward in life, they're the first steps necessary to get us from where we are and to where we desire to be. I would like to take this opportunity to echo the same to you because I want you to comprehend the significance of setting goals alongside taking aligned action.

A person without a vision for their future, is merely a person taking a walk-in life and they'll find that for the majority of the time that life happens to them instead of for them. However, a person with a vision for their life has a desired result that they envision, plans and commits to achieving and the chances are that they go on to achieve that or better. In other words, any planning you do for the future regardless of what it is, **is a goal.** So, the next time you are planning on doing the weekly chores or decide on doing something cool, always keep in mind that small tasks account as goals and while seemingly insignificant you are goal setting.

The question is are you consciously or unconsciously goal setting?

Goal setting will sharpen your focus, imagine having to shoot an arrow without being given a target.

Where would you aim?

Why would you aim there?

What is you WHY?

You can have all the potential in the world but, without the laser beam focus of a set goal your abilities and talents can go to waste.

Would you agree that sunlight cannot burn through anything without a magnifying glass focusing it, the same way that you can't achieve a goal without focusing your effort. I truly believe that setting goals help you to get back up each time you fall or lose focus. In life people often procrastinate, I believe that having a clear goal in place can help to overcome procrastination.

Once you have clarity of purpose be sure to break it down into several smaller step by step tasks to enable you to maintain progress. I enjoy setting goals because it motivates me into taking action daily. Setting goals gives you a tangible outcome to aim for and gives you something to get excited about after all it is said that it is human nature to be motived by either pain, pleasure or in some cases I feel that it is a mixture of the two. Gol setting is the source of my inspiration and motivation to move towards my desired outcome. In a nutshell, setting goals will help you to focus your energy in a positive way so that you can accomplish your desired outcomes.

So, I encourage you to create a vision board that includes all the things that you desire to achieve in the next month, three months, six months and/or twelve months.

Dreams
come true

DREAM BIG
&
MAKE IT HAPPEN

I'M THAT KID - TAKING TO THE STAGE™

I have been fortunate to grow up surrounded by world class speakers since the age of 7 years old. As a family we take our personal development very seriously, therefore we ensure that we invest our time, money and focus in improving our public speaking skills.

In my view Public Speaking is a valuable life skill that ought to be taught as young as possible because it improves confidence, I must say that public speaking has certainly helped to improve my confidence.

There are so many people in society who suffer from anxiety, public speaking skills can help you to stand tall, talk more easily and communicate in a more concise manner leaving you feeling empowered. If you are anything like I was in the past, as I use to let others do the talking for me because I found it hard to express myself.

At least until Cheryl Chapman became my coach. Rest assure because once you learn public speaking skills that will naturally fade away. Not only will you be able to fluently speak your mind but you'll find yourself doing it for others too. When you add public speaking skills to your tool box you will also have the ability to easily lead in a group and communicate in any given situation.

Public speaking training will also give you the opportunity to develop your listening, reading and writing skills as you delve into your training because in order to prepare effective speeches it will involve you practicing the ability to consider your audience which means listening carefully and sensitively to what they're saying, doing research, writing and rewriting your speech.

Public speaking will empower you to become conscious of timing, when to listen and when to pause. I really enjoy teaching others public speaking skills just as much as I enjoyed learning from my mentors. There is so much to learn about for example: storytelling, vocal variety, tonality, stance, salting, props and speech rate etc. I find that my articulation is improving too.

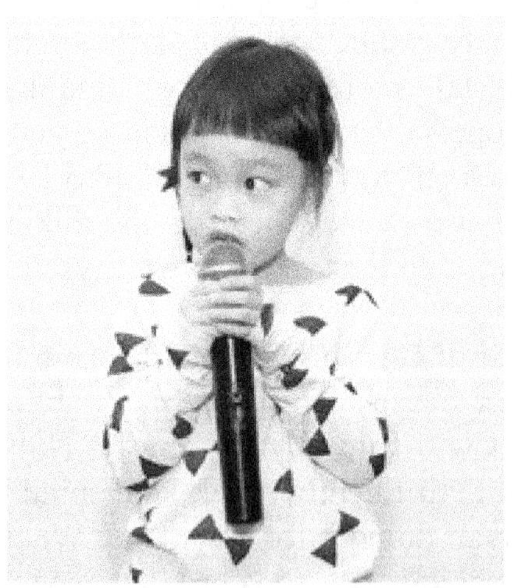

35

I'M THAT KID - INSPIRING MY COMMUNITY TO PAY IT FORWARD™

I truly believe that there are numerous benefits attached to Paying It Forward (random acts of kindness to help someone else in need).

I really enjoy being in a position to touch the hearts of others with acts of kindness. Its so fulfilling, doing good for others can have a powerful, positive effect on the immune system. It also helps me to contribute towards the greater good and in turn it has a positive impact on my self-esteem and self-worth. Acts of kindness can prevent people from becoming isolated as it encourages them to meet new people and step outside of their comfort zones.

Learn to give with a pure intention and without and hidden agenda.

it takes a village to build a legacy, so it would be a good idea to plant a seed of community cohesion today, for a brighter future tomorrow.

What can you do today to touch the heart of a stranger or someone you know?

How can you encourage others to do the same?

VOLUNTEER

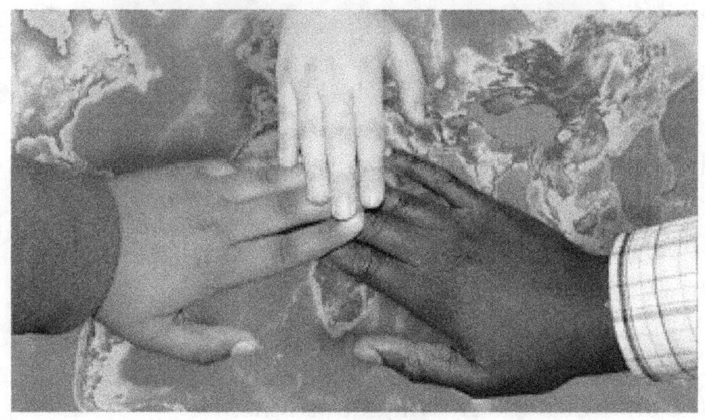

I'M THAT KID - THERE'S A BOOK INSIDE YOU™

I believe in you; I may not have met you personally however one thing that I do know is that there's a book inside you.

Writing a book is such a therapeutic process, when I am writing I find it so fascinating to see how the book writes itself one page at a time. I just love how one idea, leads to another which then allows the book to form itself. I encourage you to write a book to share your message with the world, you never know when it could lead you. I know, like I now, like I know that you have a book inside you just waiting to be shared.

Do you know what the cool thing is?

You have what it takes to inspire nations, and in exchange for your wiliness to share you will be able to publish a book for pocket money – how cool is that?

In order to write it is vital that you read books that will inspire your writing. The narrative is expanded beyond the space of the page and reading becomes a collective shared experience. Over the years I have grown to appreciate reading books that feed my mind and inspires my writing.

Now I would like you to take a note pad and pen, the answer the following questions.

The question is what are you passionate about?

What could you write about?

What title could you use?

What ten tips could you talk about easily?

Did you realise that those ten tips are the ten chapters in your book?

Now take a moment to sketch your first book cover

Who would you like to write your book foreword?

Huge congratulations for becoming an AUTHOR of your first book!!

I'M THAT KID - FAMILIES THAT PLAY TOGETHER STAY TOGETHER™

Would you agree that in today's society people seem to be busy all the time. Therefore l, it is so important to set time aside to spend quality time with family. After all, families that Play Together Stay Together. My family and I enjoy creating memories together having fun at theme parks, visiting family and friends, travelling, creating, playing games, going to the park and having family meetings etc.

Nowadays we all have busy schedules and it's as if everything is competing for our attention. This often results in us feeling tired and irritable and so much more.

This is why is vital for us to put your technological devices away and set time aside to look into each others' eyes, be present and simply play together as a family. Trust me when I say that this could be the difference that makes the difference to your family dynamics. Don't just take my work for it, at least give it a try so you can be the judge.

Roll around on the floor, play football, play a board game, chess, cards, bingo, go-karting, scramble, musical instrument, frisbee, bowling, golf or tennis. Whatever it is for you it doesn't matter what matters most is that you get to laugh together and just be playful without the distraction of technology. This will enable you to create fun memories together. I am not trying to demonise technology. In fact, I appreciate the benefit me of technology when purposefully for example you could play Nintendo Wii/Xbox Kinect family fun games. I just encourage families to take a break from whatever gets in the way of them fully connecting and looking each other in the eyes.

Do you and your family make time to eat a meal at a table together?

Do you and your family have family meetings?

Have you and your family agreed on a day for games night, movie night etc?

Do your family turn off tour technology when you go to be and/or when having a meal?

Do you and your family have a family anthem?

I encourage you to have a conversation with your family about the above.

We bond and learn through play, therefore be sure to at least try to add this important aspect to your family dynamics. Playing games helps us to relax, reduce stress and just let go of all the stresses in life.

Come up with 3 of your favourite games to play and then ask all of your family members to choose their 3 favourite games to pay.

Ask your family what they'd like to do as a family for fun.

Ask your family if you can come up with some fun things to look forward to together upon a weekly basis.

I absolutely love playing games with my family, because there's always so much laughter. We loose track of tune while having fun together and just being present. I challenge you to give your family the gift of your attention, it could be the difference that makes the difference to tour family dynamics.

I'M THAT KID - EMPOWERING YOU TO STEP INTO YOUR POWER FORMULA™

I have created a host of products and services designed to empower you to step into your power. I am extremely passionate about inspiring children and teens to learn core life skills as young as possible while having fun and generating pocket money.

I'm That KID covers:

- I'm That KID - Bridging the Gap Between Fathers & Sons™

- I'm That KID – Creating A Vision Board for My Future™

- I'm That KID – Taking the Stage™

- I'm That KID - Inspiring My Community to Pay It Forward™

- I'm That KID - There's A Book Inside ME™

- I'm That KID - Families That Play Together Stay Together™

- I'm That KID - Empowering You to Step into Your POWER™

43

- I'm That KID - BEING the Change That I Desires to See in The World™

Each one has been created with you in mind.

Did you know that we go through different stages of development? 0-7 imprint stage, 7-14 social stage, 14-21 modelling stage and 21-28 business persona stage. During each of these stages of development it's advisable to have a variety of coaches and mentors. There's a saying "You becomes the average of the five people that you spend the most time with"

Did you know that when you publish a book you become an authority within that industry? Our society is becoming more and more competitive and publishing a book gives your child the edge so they can stand out from the crowd. Your book is your business card, therefore publishing a book can be an excellent way to invest in your child's future.

Did you know that communication is the backbone of our society? It allows us to form connections, influence decisions, and motivate change. Without communication skills, the ability to progress in the working world and in life, itself, would be nearly impossible. Public speaking is one of the most important and most dreaded forms of communication

Did you know that financial education is the difference that makes the difference?

Did you know that branding is about the promises that you make and the promises that you keep?

Please see the investment options below:

DIAMOND - 4wks

EMERALD - 6wks

RUBY - 8wks

Please do not hesitate to contact me for more information.

I'M THAT KID - BEING THE CHANGE THAT I DESIRE TO SEE IN THE WORLD™

At tunes life can be filled with crowds of people in a sea of sameness. At times it's frustrating because we are conditioned at a very early age to fit it, but why fit in when you were born to stand out!

Playing small has never served anyone, least of all you. Your opinion maters, your message matters, your have something to teach and capable of learning whatever your heart desires.

You are unique, in fact you are a unique piece to the puzzle and without you the puzzle cannot be complete.

So, what would it take for you to stand a stand and be the change that you desire to see in the world?

What problems have you overcome and/or seen in the world?

What solutions do you have/can you create to some these problems?

Always remember that just because something is easy for you, doesn't mean that it's not difficult for someone else. So, learn to be the change that you want to see and aim to touch at least one people in a positive way in the hope that they'll go out and do the same.

What is your unique message to the world?

My message to the world is:

YOU ARE ENOUGH!

Come as you as you are because that's good enough.

I used to struggle with being Me because I was extremely quiet and I would be bullied for being smart. In primary school my peers would pick on me for being smart. Adults would often say that I need to be loud and bold. Deep down inside I knew that those characteristics wasn't me but I allowed other people to make me feel bad for not being like my peers. It took some time, coaching, mentoring, boos, training and a lot of experiential learning for me to finally come to the realisation that I could choose to give myself permission to simply be me, to choose to accept myself as I am, I stop allowing other people's judgements of me to dictate how I show up in the world. This is the moment when I created my first personal brand called I'm That KID which was my way of saying I'm that kids who has a passion for sports and academics and I cane up twitch this slogan "I'm That KID – I believe in myself and as long as I believe in myself I can be, do and have anything that I desire" 11yr old Tray-Sean Ben Salmi

A wonderful thing happen the day that you decide to be the change that you want to see in the world. The day I choose to be me what the day that I was saying to the world that each and every single one of us is good enough just the way we are because leaders can lead from the front the back and the middle.

If you agree with me, what decisions will you choose to make today in order to own Whi you really are, transform tour life and step into your power by becoming the change that you desire to see in the world?

Stand up for those who who are unable to stand, speak for those without a voice and be the person giving everyone else permission to be themselves.

The reason it's of vital importance to do so isn't just because it makes you more authentic, it's also because you can't change the world if you can't change yourself. As the saying goes as above so below, as within so outwards, so you see that we begin to change the world the moment that we begin to transform ourselves on the inside.

What will it take for you to plant the seed for you internal transformation?

You need to be willing to look in the mirror and learn from your reflection.

It's often easier to give advice as opposed to taking it. Always remember, no matter how I tell you – it will alerts come down to the fact that I can lead you to knowledge but I can't make you think.

I use to think that I knew too much to listen to other, until I was able to humble myself and come to the understanding that the paradox of knowledge is the more I know, the more that I realise that there is so Mubarak much more yet to comprehend because we never get complete knowing.

Get out of your own way and allow yourself to become the best version of you so you can go out there and become the change that you desire to see in the world.

It wasn't until I made the decision to start following my own advice combined with the advice of my family, mentors and coaches that my life transformed into what it is today.

 This is why I encourage you to stop pointing the finger at others, start taking responsibility for your own actions, words, and start practicing what you preach. In turn you'll grow through life and that will ultimately experiential learn to back up what you go on to teach others. It'll increase your transparency, integrity and authenticity which will ultimately make you a better leader. It'll activate your inner genius, improve your confidence and mature you in more ways than you know and it will be a fantastic way to plant the seed for your personal development. Not to mention the fact that you would be allowing yourself to learn some core life skills that you'll be able to have in your tool box.

So, you see, by choosing to be the change that you desire to see it the world is a gift to yourself and others. Not to mention that when you help others it'll be so fulfilling in way that I couldn't possibly articulate and I shall leave that to tour experiential learning.

The question is what will you choose to be, do and have with tour new expanded awareness?

CONSEQUENCES OF DELAYED CREATIVITY

I believe that there are significant consequences of delayed creativity. As it'll have a huge negative impact on your financial education, personal development, network, experiential learning, unique opportunities, pocket money and it'll deprive you of priceless experiences that you could have had.

Creativity promotes personal expression, neuroscience and cognitive science research are constantly providing information that links creativity with intelligence; academic, social, emotional intelligence; and the development of skill sets and the highest information processing that will become increasingly valuable for children and youth.

In my view allowing children to discover their unique essence of creativity as young as possible is the difference that makes the difference.

Did you know that creative expression impacts our conceptual thinking and transfer of knowledge, judgment, recognition of relationships for symbolic conceptualisation, self-evaluation of emotions, including recognising and analysing response choices and the ability to recognize and activate memories.

Take a moment to reflect on the impact that the lack of or the abundance of creativity has had on your life?

ACTION STEPS

Take a moment to reflect on all of the content that you have been exposed to in this book and then choose three *Action Steps*

1.
2.
3.

Give each *Action Steps* a deadline date

1.
2.
3.

How will you know when you have successfully achieved each of your *Action Steps*?

1.
2.
3.

Well done

EXCLUSIVE BONUS CHAPTER

There is a saying that your network equals, YOUR NET WORTH. I am certainly fortunate to be surrounded by a host of extraordinarily, phenomenal and incredible people. Therefore, I asked three of our family friends these four questions:

1.   If you were to give advice to your younger self what would it be?

2.   What are you really proud of?

3.   What would you want to change?

4.   What challenges occurred at my age (14) and what did you do to overcome them?

DR. BREMLEY W.B. LYNGDOH

*Founder and Chief Executive of Worldview Impact
Foundation*

Dr. Bremley W.B. Lyngdoh is the Founder and CEO of Worldview Impact Foundation. He is a Climate Change and Sustainable Development professional with over 20 years' experience working with Governments, IGOs, NGOs and the Private Sector developing a range of innovative projects in Asia, Africa and South America aimed at producing ecologically sound and economically viable activities that contribute directly to reducing rural poverty and generating productive sustainable livelihoods for vulnerable local communities. Bremley has all the relevant experience in project sourcing and development. His strength lies in building strategic partnerships with various governmental agencies, NGOs and multilateral development agencies. Through his previous assignments working with the United Nations and the World Bank in Asia, Africa and Latin America, he has gained expertise in the effective monitoring and evaluation of field-based programmes. Bremley developed projects on climate change adaptation, integrated agroforestry, sustainable tourism and renewable energy.

- Charity fund raising event running the Paris marathon for the Children's Trust https://www.thechildrenstrust.org.uk/
- You can support our projects by donating on http://worldviewimpact.org/causes/
- You can offset your carbon footprint by buying a rubber trees on http://worldviewimpact.com/login.php

1) If you were to give advice to your younger self what would it be?

Keep your dreams alive no matter what happens along the way and give your best each day. We need to have a powerful revolution in our hearts to create a beautiful evolution in our minds.

2) What are you really proud of?

I am very proud that Indian Prime Minister Atal Bihari Vajpayee appointed me as the Youth Representative for India during the historic United Nations Millennium Summit where I addressed world leaders during Millennium Assembly on 28th September 2000 at the UN HQ in New York.

3) What would you want to change?

If I could go back in time I would spend more time with my father in India who died from a heart attack in 2012 during his early morning run in the forest. If I had been running with him that morning I would have been able to save him and he would be still alive today.

4) What challenges occurred at my age (14) and what did you do to overcome them?

I was having challenges with balancing high school work while I was studying at St. Edmund's School in Shillong and working in my family farm to earn some pocket money. I lost my focus in time management so I joined the school musical and rebuilt my confidence by learning to perform in front of a big public audience.

JUERGEN PALLIEN

Juergen Pallien is a Master of Automation! His ability to automate success in Business and Investing creates financial liberation to pursue the most exciting and important things in life!

Juergen has used automation as the key strategy for success in his career as a serial entrepreneur, international speaker, property mogul, stock market investor and now, as a philanthropist.

Described as a Financial Liberation Genius with a Comedian's sense of humour, Juergen is on a mission to help 1 Million people achieve their own financial liberation! Educated by some of Europe's most renowned Universities in Management, Information Technology, Sales, Influence and Leadership, Juergen is fanatical about personal and professional growth and coaching. He believes that which is not growing, is dying!

Juergen is BEST known for using automation to create efficiencies in Sales, Business Growth and customer focused problem solving that led him to build and sell several companies and retire by the age of 35.

Fascinated by the stock market since he first traded in 1998, Juergen studied the investment strategies of Warren Buffett, Robert Kiyosaki and George Soros. Building on their knowledge, he has now invented several proven strategies to easily and predictably earn money without the need to sit in front of a computer all day. Juergen is committed to sharing his stock market success formulas to help One Million people put their financial success on auto-pilot and live their passion!

When he is not helping others, Juergen likes to do sports, play chess, listen to music and read lots of books.

For your questions or to learn how you can become 1 of Juergen's million beneficiaries, contact him directly at:

- YouTube: www.youtube.com/channel/UCiFeVHbloS PO0wqWZTx8gIg/videos
- Website: www.24hprofits.com
- www.facebook.com/juergen.pallien.1
- www.twitter.com/j_pallien
- www.linkedin.com/in/jpallien

1) If you were to give advice to your younger self what would it be?

Learn to invest properly and the power of compounding. Also, to only buy luxury goods and fun stuff from the earnings of your investments rather than your net worth.

2) What are you really proud of?

The results of my students who never had any experience with the stock market but tripled their investment within in the first 10 months or were able to quit their job after just 8 months.

3) What would you want to change?

Financially liberate 1 million people in the world to enable them to live their passion and make it a better place for everyone.

4) What challenges occurred at my age (14) and what did you do to overcome them?

I was living in a very small village that limited my possibilities. I'd love to help young people on their entrepreneurial journey and provide them with the knowledge and infrastructure to make their bright ideas become a reality no matter what background they have. Everyone deserves an equal chance in life.

REGAN HILLYER

Regan Hillyer is a Serial Entrepreneur, Philanthropist, Mindset Coach and Global Speaker. She is the founder of Regan Hillyer International, a company dedicated to providing personal development and business training to men and women who have a big message they want to share with the world.

Regan specializes in helping experts uncover their true message and launch powerful personal brands, helping them make a big impact and build a legacy. Regan has trained thousands of people, helping them build multiple six and seven figure businesses location free, using powerful mindset changing tools and cutting edge business development strategies.

Regan is a certified Master of NLP, Master of Hypnosis, Time Dynamics Specialist and a Success Strategist, amongst completing many other certifications and trainings. Regan has invested in excess of half a million dollars on her own personal development and business journey and takes pride in continuously learning and growing from key industry leaders.

- www.reganhillyer.com/shop

1) If you were to give advice to your younger self what would it be?

Trust yourself. Really trust yourself. All of the answers are within you and you are able to access all of these answers at any age!

2) What are you really proud of?

I'm really proud of the relationships I have in my life. My fiancé, my family relationships, my friends, my clients, my community. I am always surrounded by high vibrational people online and offline and it's taken work, but my relationships mean everything to me.

3) What would you want to change?

I'm always looking to change the number of people that I'm impacting every year.

There are so many people in the world who I want to help, and it fills me up when I am able to impact and serve at a greater level!

4) What challenges occurred at my age (14) and what did you do to overcome them?

At 14 I had no idea what I wanted to do with my life. I felt overwhelmed and confused when people asked me.

Bonus Question for my mentor:

5) What did you want to be when you grow up?

I would make up answers to try and please adults, when really, I had no idea. I went down a path of really figuring out what my purpose was in this world by diving deeper into books and personal development, and I chose to be okay with not knowing all of the answers even when people wanted me to have answers!

WHAT THE EXPERTS SAY

Feng Shui to help support children, especially those having a hard time at school by Master Sarah McAllister - a Feng Shui consultant and horoscope specialist with over 14 years experience.

A bullied kid will be suffering from fear and lack of confidence, so you really need to make sure their home environment is supportive.

Bedroom Tips to Create a Supportive Space

If possible give children separate beds, not bunk beds as they tend to feel oppressed by either the ceiling or the top bunk. Wooden bed-frames are preferable to metal ones and make sure the beds have good solid headboards. Place beds so there is a nice solid wall behind the headboard - this helps the child feel more secure. Their back is literally covered.

Study Tips

Place desks so that the chair has its back to a solid wall and child is overlooking the room or preferably looking out a window to the side too. Don't place desk against the bedroom wall to save on space, otherwise the kid is facing a brick wall, both actually and metaphorically speaking! Allow kids to study at kitchen table, as sometimes they just need to have people nearby in order to concentrate.

Respect their gut instincts

Little people have very good instincts and will know what colour they want in their room or where they want to sit to study, respect this always.

Put their artwork and pictures of friends on the bedroom wall

It sounds obvious, but some parents overlook this and leave a child's room bare and austere. Kids (and adults) **LOVE** to see images of their friends and also symbols of their success around them. Ideally place these pictures above eye level, as looking upwards activates vision and aspiration, whereas looking downwards concentrates us in the past.

Keep Electromagnetisms at a minimum in their bedroom

Electrical alarm clocks, cordless phones, mobile phones, computers - all must be either switched off or kept out of the bedroom so that the energy can settle during the night time and not interfere with the delicate bioelectrical field of your child which is still developing.

Use Natural Paints & Organic Materials if possible

Indoor air can be more polluted than outdoor air, so a good air filter is recommended, and use of natural paints. Chemical paints and artificial fabrics can create allergies in your child. The last thing they need is a skin condition or unsightly reactions due to allergies when they are already feeling vulnerable at school.

Use Chinese Horoscope Wisdom to help your child

Ask us to 'open the horoscope' of your child - we can decipher whether there is the presence of unhelpful authority (bullying) in the chart and advise colours to wear (as underwear if they have to wear a uniform), little pictures or totem animals to carry with them to support their chi, what foods are helpful to them and which directions within the house are best to occupy. *We had one mother from Croydon concerned with the amount of tickings off her son was getting at school, and my students and I went around to do a case study, moved his bed to a more empowering position and lo and almost overnight there was no more trouble. I also helped a kiddie in Holland Park to sleep through the night (previously waking up at 4am and bouncing into the parents room!) just by moving her bed to a more supportive area of the room and aligning it to 'quiet' energy as opposed to 'active' energy.*

Another young boy with Attention Deficit Disorder was immediately helped by moving the position of his bed and performing a space clearing - the father was initially sceptical but developed a respect for what I had done based on the results he had witnessed.

This type of refined, intricate and powerful classical Feng Shui is not a self-help subject - the above pointers are useful basics, but don't substitute a professional Feng Shui consultation and horoscope analysis. For further information please visit

www.myfengshuifriend.com
call 0844 848 4099 o
email info@fengshuiagency.com.

CHILDREN AND YOUTH I URGE YOU TO DREAM BIG

Having **dream**s can make you feel happy. The more important that your **dream**s are to you, the more you will want to hold on to it!!

I want you to take a moment to think about what you would do if you weren't afraid to have **FUN**, **DREAM BIG** and make **money** doing what you **LOVE**? That's right... Just go ahead and allow yourself to feel your deepest and wildest **dream**s deep within your heart. After all we all have **dream**s... right? Yes or No? Fear simply holds you back. Remember you are a *creator*, when you choose to move beyond your fears you can begin to feel free. If you don't change you can become extinct, lets face it... change is always happening.

Each and every day visualise your **dream**s as often as possible... imagine yourself enjoying your **dream**s because it can lead you to it. Movement in a new direction can help you achieve your **dream**s... so don't worry too much about being different to your peers. Difference is also good, so follow your own **dream**s and remain true to yourself. The quicker you let go of peer pressure and your old negative values and beliefs, the sooner you can find new positive values and beliefs that

will serve you well. When your values and beliefs change so will your life. It will serve you best to pursue your **dream**s instead of simply living your life in default mode following your peers etc. We both know that holding onto old negative values and beliefs will not lead you to new positive results. When you realise that you can achieve your **dream**s, your life will begin to transform if you choose to. Acknowledging small change early can help you to adept to **big**ger changes that are to come, simply allow your **dream**s to flow and then you can begin your dance with the universe.
Sabrina Ben Salmi BSc

WORDS FROM THE HEART OF A GRANDMOTHER

Parents: You have to help our children and youth, because they are tomorrow's leaders. If your child has a **dream,** you must help them to nurture that seed for it to grow. Without TLC that seed can not grow and your Childs' **dream** will surely die. It is not about pushing or pressuring your child. Ask your child how you can be of assistance and best support them to grow their **dream**? If you notice that your child is reaching out for support with a desire to be creative. Encourage them in each and every way, but always remember that it is your child's **dream** not yours. Also, too much pressure could disrupt their creative process. Take one step at a time and enjoy the experience with them. Simply embrace this priceless experience together and give them a little independence as this will help them to learn valuable life lessons along the way.

Children and Youth: If you have a **dream** don't let anyone take your **dream** away from you because that **dream** is yours and it was created by you and no one but you has the ability to breath life into your **dream**. Always believe in yourself and your **dream**s 100%. There is no such thing as too young; even if you are 5 years old give it your all. In the end at least you will know that you have at least tried your best.

Mary Paul

CONNECTING THE DOTS & GETTING STARTED

Create a table that looks like the one below using the following headings: Name, E-mail, Contact Number and Possible Support.

Name	E-mail	Contact Number	Possible Support
Nancy	nancy@hotmail.com	07510342008	Brainstorm team member
Tom	tom@wow.co.uk	07823512098	Brainstorm team member
Live Unltd	info@liveunltd.com	02075662000	Grant, mentoring etc
May	may@ya.co.uk	07795551232	Website & business card designs
Mum/ Dad	Mum&dad@home.com	07777251982	Practical and moral support

Once you have completed this promise to make contact with each individual listed and talk to them about your **dream**s. Clearly explain the possible support which they can give you and more importantly offer to assist them in some way.

BOOKS:

- How to Be A Student Entrepreneur by Junior Ogunyemi
- Rich Dad, Poor Dad for Teens by Robert Kiyosaki
- Conversations with God for teens By Neale Donald Walsch
- The Little Soul and The Sun by Neale Donald Walsch
- The Little Soul and The Earth by Neale Donald Walsch
- Raising CEO Kids by Dr Jerry Cook & Sarah Cook
- Who moved my cheese by Dr Spencer Johnson
- Think and Grow Rich by Napoleon Hill
- Key Person of Influence by Daniel Precisely
- The Secret by Rhonda Byrne
- The Hidden Messages in Water by Dr Masaru Emoto
- I THINK I AM by Louise L. Hay
- The Story of The Ethical Elephants by Catherine Warrington

DVDs:

- The Secret
- What the Bleep Do You Know?
- Thrive

OTHER RESOURCES:

- Building Brands: www.buildingbrands.com
- Marketing File: www.marketingfile.com
- Fiverr: www.fiverr.com
- Survey Monkey: www.surveymonkey.com
- Cision PR & Communications: www.cision.com
- British Library Business & IP Centre: www.bl.uk/bipc
- CEO Email Addresses: www.ceoemail.com
- Clearlyso: www.clearlyso.com
- Grant Finder: www.grantfinder.co.uk
- BERR: www.berrgov.uk
- Unity Node: www.unitynode.org
- Talking IT Global: www.tigweb.org
- NBAN: www.nban.co.uk
- HMRC national advice service: www.hmrc.gov.uk
- Money Facts: www.moneyfacts.co.uk
- Apprenticeships: www.apprenticeships.org.uk
- 365 Tickets: www.365tickets.com
- Merlin Annual Pass: www.merlinannualpass.com
- Family Railcard: www.familyandriends-railcrad.co.uk
- East London Business Alliance: www.elba-1.org.uk
- British Dyslexia Association: www.bdadyslexiaorg.uk

- Mansa the high IQ society:
  www.mensa.org.uk
- Unltd: www.unltd.org.uk
- Khan Academy: www.khanacademy.org
- Starfall: www.starfall.com
- **Lashai Ben Salmi:
  www.lashaibensalmi.com &
  www.lashaibensalmi.co.uk
  info@kidzthatdreambig.com**
- Book Trust: www.booktrust.org.uk
- Peter Jones: www.peterjones.tv
- Urban Unlimited: www.uunetwork.co.uk
- Bright Ideas: www.brightideastrust.com
- Livity: www.livity.co.uk
- So, You Wanna Be In TV?:
  www.soyouwannabeintv.com
- Shell Livewire: www.shell-livewire.org
- Bold Achievers Club:
  www.boldachieversclub.com
- School for Startups:
  www.schoolforstartups.co.uk
- Young Entreprenur Society:
  www.youngentrepreneursociety.org.uk
- UK Intellectual Property Office:
  www.patent.gov.uk
- Waterlow Legal:
  www.chambersdirectory.co.uk
- Get British Business Online:
  www.gbbo.co.uk
- Business in The Community:
  www.bitc.org.uk
- The Prince's Trust: www.princes-
  trust.org.uk

- Your Hidden Potential:
  www.yourhiddenpotential.co.uk
- Raising CEO Kids:
  www.raisingceokids.com
- The Secret: www.thesecret.tv

Sponsors **we appreciate all of the advice, support, opportunities and so much more that we get from you all:**

- Dawn Gibbins: www.dawngibbins.com
- Lime Tree: www.limetreeonline.com
- Andrew Sage: www.asae.co.uk.com
- Froggo Marketing:
  www.froggomarketing.co.uk
- Robert G. Allen: www.robertgallen.com
- Live Unltd: www.liveunltd.com
- Sabrina Ben Salmi (Mother) :
  www.sabrinabensalmi.co.uk
- Mary Paul (Grandmother):
  www.wowthankyou.com/marypaulscreatio
  ns
- Junior Ogunyemi:
  www.linkedin.com/pub/junior-
  ogunyemi/1a/123/305
- Alex Browning: www.alexbrowning.tv
- ClearlySo: www.clearlyso.com

Trust yourself, as you k**now** more than you think you do. Simply inhale inspiration and exhale action. **G**o ahead and do what you k**now** you ought to do. The answer you have always been waiting for is yes you can, do, be and have whatever your heart desires.

It is an absolute honour to welcome you to the family.

What are you going to do to celebrate your achievements?

((((CONGRATULATIONS))))

ABOUT THE AUTHOR

AS SEEN OF TV, RADIO & NEWSPAPERS
Tray-Sean Ben Salmi aka I'm That KID is not your average 14yr old. Tray-Sean Ben Salmi is a 14yr old Amazon No.1 Award Winning Author, Public Speaker Award Winning, Presented award for TruLittle Heros Award 2018, Guest Speaker at The Beat You Expo, Multi-award winning child advocate, Made For Mums Judge 2018, former member of Team Trouble (participated in campaigns for Sainsburys, Legoland, Warner Bros, Sony and Made For Mums to name a few) founded by Shadia Daho, Amazing Arabella & JD The Super Car Kid, Child Genius 2017 1 of 20 smartest children in the UK, 1 of 34 boys invited to sit at the prestigious Eton College for Boys. Official Judge for Made For Mums Toy Awards 2018 via Team Trouble, An award winning author of Kidz That Dream Big, Former Radio Show host, Regan Hillyer International Be Your Brand Fellow, Author of 10 Seconds To Child Genius, Winner of TruLittle Heros Award - Academic 2017, Public speaker, a business/personal developments mentor & coach and founder of I'm That KID Blueprint covers:

- I'm That KID - Bridging the Gap Between Fathers & Sons
- I'm That KID – Creating A Vision Board for My Future
- I'm That KID – Taking to The Stage
- I'm That KID - Inspiring My Community to Pay It Forward

- I'm That KID - There's A Book Inside ME
- I'm That KID - Families That Play Together, Stay Together
- I'm That KID - Empowering You to Step into Your POWER
- I'm That KID - BEING the Change That I Desires to See in The World

And co-founder of 10 Seconds to Child Genius who is here to help child to plant the seed to create a brighter Future. Tray-Sean's signature program: I'M That KID Blueprint™

BEN SALMI FAMILY MANTRA

"BEN SALMI TEAMWORK, MAKES THE DREAMWORK

We believe that there is no such thing as failure only feedback.

We also believe that the journey of one thousand miles begins with a single step in the right direction

FAMILY ANTHEM
If you want to be somebody,
If you want to go somewhere,
You better wake up and PAY ATTENTION
I'm ready to be somebody,
I'm ready to go somewhere,
I'm ready to wake up and PAY ATTENTION!

The question is *ARE YOU?*

ABOUT TRAY-SEAN'S SIBLINGS

AS SEEN OF TV, RADIO & NEWSPAPERS
Lashai Ben Salmi aka DREAMPRENEUR is not your average 18yr old. She is a multi-award winning Youth Advocate, Presented award for TruLittle Heros Award 2018, Content Creator for The Korean Cultural Centre, Winner of TruLittle Heros Award - Entreprenur 2017, Speaker at Virgin Money Lounge Historical Black History Month first ever event, Guest Speaker at The Beat You Expo, Guest Speaker at Mercedes Benz World 10th April 2018, High Profile Club, YouTuber with 25K plus subscribers and over 4M plus views (Korean Channel), An award winning author of Kidz That Dream Big, Andy Harrington ACE Coach, Former International Radio Show host, Winner of Regan Hillyer International Scholarship, a speaker, a business/personal developments mentor & coach, founder of Blossom Tree Photography & Videography (Produced content for Shadia Daho for Amazing Arabella, JD The Super Kid & Team Trouble in association with Legoland Resort, Harry Potter, Little Mix and Disney Pixar, Sony, Warner Brothers & Universal etc) co-founder of A Precipice of A Dream and founder of Put The RED Card Up To bullying & My Journey - Giving Youth Several Reasons to Smile who is here to help children and youth to plant the seed for an abundance of unique opportunities via a variety of products and services to assist you to create a brighter future

Lashai has been mentored by some of the leading name within the personal development world Regan Hillyer, Andy Harrington, Cheryl Chapman, Harry Singha, Ralph Plumb, Sammy Blindell to name a few. Lashai has shared the stage with the likes of the late Dr Miles Monrune, Dr John Demartini, Andy Harrington, Robert G Allen and Ralph Plumb to name a few.

If you are looking for an inspiring, wise, talented, refreshing and powerful speaker then 18yr old Lashai Ben Salmi is guaranteed to make a big impact at your event. Lashai has been a part of the personal development world since the age of 11yrs. Lashai has a burning desire to transform lives with her stage presence, knowledge and wisdom! Lashai's signature topics include: Congruency, Alignment, Self-Belief, YouTube, Social Media, Connection, Inspiration and Motivation.

Lashais signature program: The Stepping Stone's Formula™

Book: Kidz That Dream Big: Dreams Do Come True
https://www.amazon.co.uk/dp/1912547066/ref=cm_sw_r_cp_api_mwbUAbS8BTQHE

Facebook page: Kidz That Dream Big:
https://www.facebook.com/Kidz-that-Dream-BIG-154694734627138/

AS SEEN OF TV, RADIO & NEWSPAPERS

Yasmine Ben Salmi is not your average 11yr old. Yasmine Ben Salmi aka LovePreneur is an 11yr award winning author of The Choice is Your - 10 Keys Principles To Create A Happier Lifestyle, Winner of TruLittle Heros Award - Creative 2017, Guest Speaker at The Beat You Expo, Former International Radio Show Host, Member of Team Trouble (participated in campaigns for Sainsburys, Legoland, Warner Bros, Sony and Made For Mums to name a few) founded by Amazing Arabella & JD The Super Car Kid, Yasmines signature program: Your Thinking C.A.P For Living & Loving Life™, Yasmine's Dog Walking Service "Woof-Woof your dog is here", Nominated for a R.E.E.B.A Award 2017, Winner of Radio Works Authors Awards 2017, Nominated for National Diversity Award 2017, founder of Mother and Daughter Connect Collection and founder of Lovepreneur.

Book: The Choice Is Yours: 10 Key Principles to Create a Happier Lifestyle
https://www.amazon.co.uk/dp/1912547082/ref=cm_sw_r_cp_api_JbaUAbR7K3MNS

Facebook page: Lovepreneur:
https://m.facebook.com/YasmineBenSalmiakaLovePrenur/

AS SEEN OF TV, RADIO & NEWSPAPERS

9yr old Paolo Ben Salmi aka Pint Size Adventurer is not is not your average 9yr old. Paolo is Water-to-Go's youngest ever ambassador! https://www.watertogo.eu/paolobensalmi blog about Water-to-Go and Paolo: https://www.watertogo.eu/blog/meet-paolo-water-to-gos-youngest-ever-ambassador/ Paolo Ben Salmi is an award winning author of Pint Size Adventurer - 10 Keys Principles To Get Your KIDS off their iPads & Into The Wild, Award Winning Public Speaker (who has spoken at eleventh such as Mercedes Benz World), Former member of Team Trouble (participated in campaigns for Sainsburys, Legoland, Warner Bros, Sony and Made For Mums to name a few) founded by Amazing Arabella & JD The Super Car Kid, Paolo's signature program is called The Abundant Adventure Inventor™, 2nd place in TruLittle Heros Award - U12 Entrepreneur 2017, Guest Speaker at The Beat You Expo, Mercedes Benz World 10th April, Official Judge for Made For Mums Toy Awards 2018 via Team Trouble, Former International Radio Show host, 229/17 Paolo made history by being the youngest to interview Dr John Demartini: https://www.facebook.com/350400542063654/videos/363072487463126/, personal developments coach and founder of Pint Size Adventurer who is here to help you to plant the seed toward self-discovery, exploration of the internal and external world and adventurer in abundance via a variety of products and services to assist you to create a brighter future

Book: Pint Size Adventurer: 10 Key Principles to Get Your KIDS off Their iPads & Into the Wild

https://www.amazon.co.uk/dp/1912547031/ref=cm
_sw_r_cp_api_iwXXAbMZRM7QA

Facebook page: Pint Size Adventurer:
https://m.facebook.com/paolobensalmiakapintsizea
dventurer/

AS SEEN OF TV, RADIO & NEWSPAPERS
Amire Ben Salmi is not your average 5yr old. Amire
Ben Salmi aka Mr Because I AM Intelligent is a 5yr
old award winning author of Because I AM
Intelligent - 365 Affirmations To Brighten Up Your
Day, Guest Speaker at The Beat You Expo, Member
of Team Trouble (participated in campaigns for
Sainsburys, Legoland, Warner Bros and Sony to
name a few) founded by Amazing Arabella & JD
The Super Car Kid, Amire's signature program is
Easy-As-P.I.E™ and He's founder of Because I
AM Intelligent who is here to help you to plant the
seed toward having fun learning during childhood,
Positive Affirmations, Fun and Creativity in
abundance via a variety of products such as a book
with a matching colour car and 52 affirmation cards
to assist you to create a brighter future

Book: Because I AM Intelligent 365 Affirmations
to Brighten Up Your Day
https://www.amazon.co.uk/dp/1912547023/ref=cm
_sw_r_cp_api_gcaUAb6A5W5SJ

Facebook page: Because I AM Intelligent:
https://m.facebook.com/BecauseIAMIntelligent/

KEEP IN TOUCH VIA SOCIAL MEDIA

FACEBOOK: I'm That Kid
TWITTER: @traybensalmi
INSTAGRAM: authortrayseanbensalmi
LINKEDIN: Tray-Sean Ben Salmi

Please do not hesitate to contact me

BE WITH WHO MAKES
YOU SMILE
LAUGH AS MUCH
AS YOU BREATHE
LOVE AS LONG
AS YOU LIVE
I'M THAT
KID

FRANCE
FRANCE
10
FRANCE

Forbes Entrepreneur CBS FOX NBC StarTribune The Boston Globe THE WASHINGTON POST
10 SECONDS
TO CHILD GENIUS
From Eton Road To Eton College
BEST
AWARD
Tray-Sean Ben Salmi
Author, Speaker &
Coach
Regan Hillyer
Speaker, Coach,
Multi Millionaire
ETRO BANK sky the Recorder BBC RADIO 1 6 THE BIG ISSUE UnLtd THE BEST YOU EXPO

FIRSTPOINT

Parent & Carer conference
Educating, empowering, encouraging, bringing security & support to children & their family unit.
1st June 2019
2pm - 4:30pm
THEME
TIME OF STRENGTHENING.
WITH A SPECIAL VISIT FROM THE MAYOR OF HAVERING
OUR GUEST SPEAKERS
DISCUSSION OF EXPLORATION
Dreaming Big Together as a Family
MEET OUR MENTAL HEALTH PANEL!
Do you know that over 80% of persons with diagnosable mental illness are not known to services?
Do you know that mental illness is the biggest illness of burden on the NHS?
Join our panel of discussants on Mental Wellbeing
PERFORMANCES
ARIANNA HORGAN
ADAM RICHARD
VENUE
Queens Theatre
Billet Ln, Hornchurch
RM11 1QT
PACE   TESCO   SYNERGIED

"I'M THAT KID"

"I'M THAT
KID"
By Tray-Sean Ben Salmi

abc
Forbes
Entrepreneur
CBS
FOX
NBC
StarTribune
The Boston Globe
THE HUFFINGTON POST
10 SECONDS
TO CHILD GENIUS
From Eton Road To Eton College
TRAY-SEAN BEN SALMI
BEST SELLING
AWARD winning AUTHOR
Tray-Sean Ben Salmi
Author, Speaker &
Coach
A huge congratulations
to Tray-Sean for
publishing his new book
Regan Hillyer
Speaker, Coach,
Multi-Millionaire
METRO
SKY
Ilford Recorder
BBC RADIO
THE BIG ISSUE
UnLtd
THE BEST YOU

10 SECONDS TO CHILD GENIUS
amazon.com BEST SELLING AUTHOR
AS SEEN ON TV, RADIO, NEWSPAPERS AND MAGAZINES
INFLUENCER
TRAY-SEAN BEN SALMI
13yr old Tray-Sean Ben Salmi aka
"I'm That KID"
(Award winner & Channel 4
Child Genius Participant)
&
PHILIP CHAN
"10-Seconds Maths Expert"
Awards-Winning Authors

I
INFLUENCER
PUBLISHING

money
Luster's PRODUCTS INC.

MKHSA
HAIR STUDIO & ACADEMY
www.mkhsa.co.uk

KIDZ THAT
DREAM
BIG
KIDZ THAT
DREAM
BIG
"DREAMS DO COME TRUE"
LASHAI BEN SALMI & TRAY-SEAN BEN SALMI

DISCLAIMER

Tray-Sean Ben Salmi (the author) is a business and life coach/mentor. Nothing more and nothing less. The Author cannot, and do not, make any promises, guarantees, warrantees or representations about results other than the coaches diligent work with you. Advices are being provided "AS IS" without warranty of any kind, either express or implied, including without limitation any warranty for information, coaching, products or services provided through or in connection with this book. The advices in this book are requested at the coaching/mentoring participant's own choice and with inherent singular responsibility of the coaching/mentoring participant.

The author would like to explicitly point out that the advices that the author offer do not replace the expertise of a medical doctor or of an alternative non-medicine practitioner. Advices differ decidedly from those of a medical doctor or that of a practitioner in the non-medical area.

The author does not claim to make any diagnosis or give any promises of any sort of healing processes. The author is neither qualified nor equipped to deal with a person with pathological history, should you be in medical or psychiatric treatment due to any health issues, it is strongly advised to continue your therapy with your doctors. In case you still want to be coached/mentored by the author of this book, kindly consult your doctors before contacting the author. Whatever your decision, please do not interrupt your treatment with your doctor(s).
This book is focused on offering you a host of inspiration and resources to give you a chance to open your mind to the wonders of abundance in life for a more satisfying existence. This book will help you to learn how to loosen the control mechanisms that habitually stop us. For all other physical or mental health issues you are advised to consult professionals who are specifically trained to treat such challenges.

The author shall not be responsible for any loss or damage caused, or alleged to have been caused, directly or indirectly, by the information or ideas contained, suggested, or referenced in this book. However, if any legal relations arise in connection with this book, shall be governed by and construed in accordance with the laws of United Kingdom.